D0376850

by Astrid Lindgren
& Ingrid Vang Nyman
translated by Tiina Nunnally

Astrid Lindgren's

Pippi

The Strongest in the World!

PIPPI
LONGSTOCKING
MOVES IN
A. LINDGREN & VANG

WHAT SHOULD WE DO, TOMMY?
I DON'T KNOW. THERE'S NOTHING FUN TO DO.
THIS IS THE PRETTY HOUSE WHERE TOMMY AND ANNIKA LIVE.

NEXT DOOR TO TOMMY AND ANNIKA THERE'S AN EMPTY HOUSE. NOBODY LIVES THERE.

IT'S SO STUPID THAT NOBODY LIVES THERE.
YEAH, SOMEONE SHOULD MOVE IN. SOMEONE WITH KIDS.

CAN YOU BELIEVE IT, ANNIKA? SHE'S LIFTING A HORSE!
NOBODY CAN LIFT A HORSE!
I CAN.
ONE NIGHT, A LITTLE GIRL MOVES INTO THE EMPTY HOUSE. TOMMY AND ANNIKA DON'T KNOW IT YET, BUT SHE'S THE STRONGEST IN THE WORLD.

WHAT'S YOUR NAME?
I'M PIPPI LONGSTOCKING.
PIPPI LONGSTOCKING? THAT'S NOT A REAL NAME.
OF COURSE IT IS. WHAT ARE YOUR NAMES?

WE'RE TOMMY AND ANNIKA.
WHY IS THERE A HORSE ON YOUR PORCH?

WELL, HE WOULDN'T BE HAPPY IN THE LIVING ROOM AND HE'D JUST GET IN THE WAY IN THE KITCHEN.

YOU'RE SO LUCKY TO HAVE A MONKEY. WHAT'S HIS NAME?
THIS IS MR. NILSSON. COME ON, LET'S GO INSIDE.

WHERE ARE YOUR MOTHER AND FATHER?
GONE. GONE FAR AWAY.
BUT WHO ON EARTH LOOKS AFTER YOU?

THAT'S RIGHT. PIPPI LIVES ALL BY HERSELF IN VILLA VILLEKULLA, AND SHE THINKS THAT'S JUST FINE.

WHEN PIPPI MAKES PANCAKES, SHE TOSSES THE EGGS HIGH IN THE AIR. ONE EGG LANDS ON HER HEAD.

EAT FAST, AND THEN WE'LL GO IN THE LIVING ROOM.

WHAT'S IN THAT DESK?
TREASURES. BIRD EGGS AND MIRRORS AND PEARL NECKLACES AND STUFF. I'M GOING TO GIVE YOU BOTH PRESENTS.

TOMMY GETS A NICE DAGGER WITH A MOTHER-OF-PEARL HILT. ANNIKA GETS A LITTLE BOX WITH PINK SHELLS ON THE LID. INSIDE IS A RING WITH A GREEN STONE.

YOU'D BETTER LEAVE NOW BECAUSE IF YOU DON'T GO HOME, YOU CAN'T COME BACK, AND THAT WOULD BE A SHAME.
THANKS, PIPPI! YOU'RE THE BEST!
AND THE STRONGEST, TOO.

BYE, PIPPI. WE'LL BE BACK TOMORROW.
AND EVERY DAY AFTER THAT.
SEE YOU SOON!
TOMMY AND ANNIKA GO HOME, HAPPY TO HAVE A NEW PLAYMATE.

A. LINDGREN & VANG
PIPPI
LONGSTOCKING
IS A THING-
SEARCHER

TOMMY, WAKE UP! LET'S SEE
WHAT PIPPI'S DOING TODAY.

PIPPI ALWAYS ROLLS OUT HER
GINGERSNAPS ON THE FLOOR.
STOP WALKING ON
THE DOUGH, MR. NILSSON!

HOW NICE OF YOU TO DROP BY!

WHAT ARE WE GOING
TO DO TODAY, PIPPI?
I DON'T KNOW WHAT YOU'RE DOING,
BUT I'M A THING-SEARCHER, SO
I DON'T HAVE A MINUTE TO SPARE.

A THING-SEARCHER? WHAT'S THAT?
SOMEBODY WHO SEARCHES FOR THINGS, OF COURSE.

WHAT KIND OF THINGS?
ALL SORTS OF THINGS. GOLD NUGGETS AND OSTRICH FEATHERS AND DEAD RATS AND TINY LITTLE SCREWS AND THINGS LIKE THAT.

CAN WE BE THING-SEARCHERS, TOO?
SURE, WHY NOT? BUT WE'D BETTER HURRY, OR SOME OTHER THING-SEARCHER WILL TAKE ALL THE GOLD NUGGETS.

DO WE GET TO KEEP EVERYTHING WE FIND?
YES, EVERYTHING ON THE GROUND.

HE'S LYING ON THE GROUND, AND WE'VE FOUND HIM. TAKE HIM!
BUT, PIPPI, WE CAN'T TAKE A GROWN MAN!
IF YOU SAY SO. BUT IT BOTHERS ME THAT ANOTHER THING-SEARCHER MIGHT COME ALONG AND SWIPE HIM.

WHAT A FIND! YOU CAN NEVER HAVE TOO MANY TIN CANS.
WHAT WILL YOU USE IT FOR?

YOU CAN PUT IT OVER YOUR HEAD AND PRETEND IT'S THE MIDDLE OF THE NIGHT.

BONK

IMAGINE IF I WASN'T WEARING THIS CAN! I MIGHT HAVE FALLEN ON MY FACE AND REALLY HURT MYSELF.

OH, LOOK WHAT I FOUND. A SWEET LITTLE WOODEN SPOOL FOR BLOWING SOAP BUBBLES.
BUT TOMMY AND I HAVEN'T FOUND ANYTHING.

WHY DON'T YOU GO LOOK INSIDE THAT OLD TREE STUMP? TREE STUMPS ARE SOME OF THE BEST PLACES FOR A THING-SEARCHER TO LOOK.

WOW! A NICE LITTLE NOTEBOOK!
AND A PEN!

AND LOOK WHAT I FOUND: A CORAL NECKLACE!
SEE? DIDN'T I TELL YOU? THERE'S NOTHING BETTER THAN BEING A THING-SEARCHER.

JUST THINK HOW STUPID PEOPLE ARE. THEY ARE CARPENTERS AND SHOEMAKERS AND CHIMNEY-SWEEPS, BUT NO ONE IS EVER A THING-SEARCHER. AND IT'S SUCH A GREAT JOB.

NONE OF THE GROWN-UPS IN THAT SMALL TOWN THOUGHT A LITTLE GIRL COULD LIVE ON HER OWN. THEY SENT TWO POLICEMEN TO TAKE PIPPI TO A CHILDREN'S HOME.

I HOPE THE KID IS HOME SO WE CAN TAKE HER WITH US RIGHT AWAY.

HERE COME TWO POLICEMEN!

WHAT LUCK! POLICEMEN ARE MY SECOND FAVORITE THING, AFTER RHUBARB PUDDING.

ARE YOU THE LITTLE GIRL WHO HAS MOVED INTO VILLA VILLEKULLA?

NOPE. I'M A LITTLE OLD WOMAN WHO LIVES ON THE OTHER SIDE OF TOWN.

DON'T BE FUNNY. TELL US YOUR NAME.

PIPPILOTTA VICTUALIA WINDOWSHADE CURLYMINT EPHRAIMSDAUGHTER LONGSTOCKING.

MY DEAR PIPPI LONGSTOCKING. WE'RE SUPPOSED TO TAKE YOU TO A CHILDREN'S HOME.

BUT I ALREADY HAVE ONE. I'M A CHILD AND THIS IS MY HOME. SO THIS IS A CHILDREN'S HOME.

A CHILD CAN'T LIVE ALONE.
REALLY? CAN I BRING MY HORSE TO YOUR CHILDREN'S HOME?

NO, OF COURSE NOT.
THEN YOU'LL HAVE TO FIND KIDS FOR YOUR CHILDREN'S HOME SOMEWHERE ELSE. I'M NOT GOING.

DON'T YOU REALIZE YOU HAVE TO GO TO SCHOOL AND LEARN YOUR MULTIPLICATION TABLES?
I DON'T THINK I NEED ANY PLUTIFICATION TABLES.

YOU'RE COMING WITH US. RIGHT NOW.

OH, WHAT FUN! SHALL WE PLAY TAG?

THAT GIRL IS CRAZY. SHE'S CLIMBING UP ON THE ROOF!
QUICK! WE HAVE TO CATCH HER.

HERE I GO!

ARE YOU STUCK?
DO YOU THINK I'VE GOT MY LEG IN THE CHIMNEY JUST FOR THE FUN OF IT?

YOU NAUGHTY CHILD, PUT BACK THAT LADDER!
WHY ARE YOU SO MAD? DON'T YOU LIKE TAG?

WE HAVE TO PRETEND TO BE NICE, OTHERWISE WE'LL NEVER GET DOWN.
PLEASE PUT BACK THE LADDER, DEARIE.

THAT'S MORE LIKE IT.

HA HA.
YOU DESERVE A SPANKING.

DIDN'T YOU KNOW THAT PIPPI'S THE STRONGEST IN THE WORLD?
I DON'T HAVE TIME TO PLAY TAG ANYMORE.

A. LINDGREN & VANG
PIPPI
GOES TO SCHOOL
LOOK HOW SHE'S SLEEPING!
WHY DOES SHE HAVE HER FEET ON THE PILLOW?

BECAUSE THAT'S HOW THEY SLEEP IN GUATEMALA. AND THEY SLEEP SO SOUNDLY.

PIPPI, WHY DON'T YOU COME WITH US TO SCHOOL?
WHY WOULD I DO THAT?
YOU WOULDN'T BELIEVE WHAT A NICE TEACHER WE HAVE.

AND YOU DON'T HAVE TO BE THERE VERY LONG.
AND THEN YOU'LL HAVE VACATION AT CHRISTMAS AND EASTER AND IN THE SUMMER.
THAT'S SO UNFAIR. I WON'T PUT UP WITH IT.

WHAT DO YOU MEAN?
JUST BECAUSE I DON'T GO TO SCHOOL, I DON'T GET TO HAVE CHRISTMAS VACATION.

SO THE VERY NEXT DAY, PIPPI RODE OFF TO SCHOOL.

HI GUYS.
AM I IN TIME FOR PLUTIFICATION?

WELCOME! I HOPE YOU'LL LIKE IT HERE AND LEARN A LOT.
AND I HOPE I GET A CHRISTMAS VACATION.

WOULD YOU TELL US YOUR NAME?
PIPPILOTTA VICTUALIA WINDOWSHADE CURLYMINT EPHRAIMSDAUGHTER LONGSTOCKING.
BUT EVERYBODY JUST CALLS ME PIPPI.

ALL RIGHT, PIPPI DEAR, LET'S SEE IF YOU CAN ADD. HOW MUCH IS FIVE PLUS SEVEN?
SHOULDN'T YOU ALREADY KNOW THAT?
YOU CAN'T TALK TO THE TEACHER LIKE THAT.

THE TEACHER IS WORN OUT FROM TRYING TO HELP PIPPI ADD AND READ.

ALL RIGHT. EVERYBODY STAND UP. WE'RE GOING TO SING A SONG.
GO AHEAD AND SING. I'M GOING TO TAKE A NAP. TOO MUCH LEARNING CAN WEAR A PERSON OUT.

ANYONE WHO BEHAVES AS BADLY AS YOU DO CAN'T GO TO SCHOOL.
HAVE I BEHAVED BADLY? I DIDN'T MEAN TO. I'M AWFULLY SORRY.

MAYBE YOU CAN COME BACK TO SCHOOL WHEN YOU'RE A LITTLE OLDER AND MORE SENSIBLE.
THANK YOU! WHAT A NICE TEACHER YOU ARE. HERE'S A GOLD WATCH AS A GIFT.

I'LL TAKE THE SCHOOLS IN ARGENTINA ANY DAY. YOU SHOULD GO THERE. EASTER VACATION STARTS THREE DAYS AFTER CHRISTMAS VACATION, AND WHEN EASTER IS OVER, IT'S ONLY THREE DAYS UNTIL SUMMER VACATION. BYE GUYS!

PIPPI
GOES TO THE
CIRCUS
A. LINDGREN & VANG

HAPPY BIRTHDAY, DEAR HORSIE! I HOPE YOU LIKE YOUR BEAUTIFUL BIRTHDAY BOWS.

PIPPI, PIPPI, WANT TO GO TO THE CIRCUS?
WHAT'S A SIRKUS? DOES IT HURT?

IT DOESN'T HURT! THERE ARE HORSES AND CLOWNS AND LOVELY LADIES WALKING THE TIGHTROPE.
BUT IT COSTS MONEY.

I'M AS RICH AS A TROLL, SO I CAN BUY A SIRKUS.
I CAN ALWAYS PILE UP THE CLOWNS IN THE LAUNDRY ROOM.
YOU DON'T HAVE TO BUY THE CIRCUS, SILLY.

PIPPI JUMPS RIGHT ONTO THE HORSE'S BACK.

GET OFF, YOU NAUGHTY GIRL!
SIMMER DOWN! YOU'RE NOT THE ONLY ONE ALLOWED TO HAVE FUN.

IT'S OKAY, I CAN RIDE AGAIN ANOTHER DAY.

THE RINGMASTER SENT TWO MEN OVER TO THROW PIPPI OUT—BUT THEY COULDN'T BUDGE HER.
YOU MIGHT AS WELL GIVE UP. YOU'LL JUST RUIN YOUR NAILS.

HERE IS MISS ELVIRA, TIGHTROPE WALKER!

WALK THE TIGHTROPE? I CAN DO THAT, TOO.

WHAT'S THE MATTER? AREN'T WE HAVING FUN?
COME DOWN, YOU AWFUL CHILD!

NOT EVERYBODY CAN TICKLE THEIR EAR WHILE WALKING THE TIGHTROPE.

HURRAY!
HURRAY FOR PIPPI!
THREE CHEERS FOR PIPPI LONGSTOCKING!

LOOK OUT BELOW!

YOU'RE THE BEST HORSE! BUT WHERE ARE YOUR BOWS?

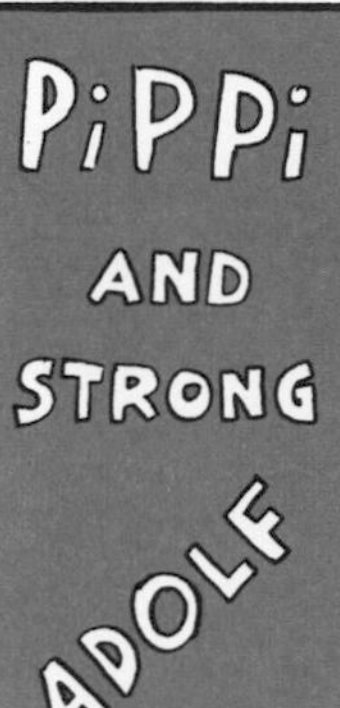

AFTER PIPPI WALKED THE TIGHTROPE, THE CIRCUS RINGMASTER WAS MAD ENOUGH TO BURST. BUT HE HAD TO CALM DOWN.

GO! GET LOST! OUT OF MY SIGHT!
WHY ARE YOU ALWAYS SO UNFRIENDLY? I JUST WANT TO FIGHT WITH STRONG ADOLF.
200

LET'S GET STARTED.

YAY, PIPPI!
YAY, PIPPI!

100

TIDDLY-POM AND PIDDLY-DEE.

ALL RIGHT, LITTLE MAN. THAT'S ENOUGH FOR NOW.

IT CAN'T GET ANY MORE FUN THAN THIS.

THANKS, BUT I HAVE MY OWN MONEY. USE IT FOR FRIED HERRING IF YOU LIKE.
IF YOU'RE SURE, BUT YOU DID WIN FAIR AND SQUARE.
100

THREE CHEERS FOR MISS LONGSTOCKING, THE STRONGEST IN THE WORLD!
YES, THAT'S EXACTLY WHAT I AM.

PIPPI GOES SHOPPING
WHAT SHOULD WE DO TODAY, PIPPI?
WE COULD GO SKATING, EXCEPT THAT THE ICE MELTED A LONG TIME AGO.

I KNOW WHAT WE'LL DO. LET'S WALK TO TOWN AND GO SHOPPING.

I LIKE DITCHES. I'M PRETENDING TO BE A BOAT.
ON THE WAY TO TOWN, PIPPI FOUND A DITCH.

I MEAN, A SUBMARINE.

BUT NOW YOU'RE SOAKING WET.
SO? WHAT'S WRONG WITH THAT?

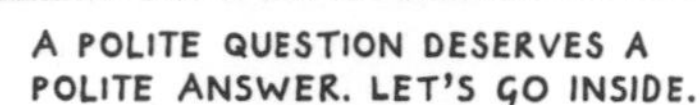
A POLITE QUESTION DESERVES A POLITE ANSWER. LET'S GO INSIDE.

DO YOU SUFFER FROM FRECKLES ?

NO, I DON'T SUFFER FROM FRECKLES. I LIKE THEM.

PIPPI, SHOULD WE GO IN THIS SHOP?
YES, LET'S GO IN. WAY IN.

I'D LIKE FORTY POUNDS OF CANDY. AND COULD I HAVE SIXTY LOLLIPOPS AND SEVENTY BAGS OF TOFFEE? AND I DON'T THINK I'LL NEED MORE THAN ONE HUNDRED AND THREE CHOCOLATE-CHIP COOKIES TODAY.

IF THERE ARE ANY KIDS HERE WHO DON'T EAT CANDY, PLEASE STEP FORWARD...NOBODY? TOMMY, OPEN THE BAGS!

NOW LET'S GO INTO THE NEXT SHOP.

HOW MAY I HELP YOU?
YOU CAN HELP US WITH A LITTLE OF EVERYTHING. FOR STARTERS, WE'RE OUT OF WHISTLES.

DID ALL THE KIDS GET THE TOYS THEY WANTED? IF SO, THEN I'M GOING TO THE DRUGSTORE.
BUT PIPPI, YOU'RE NOT SICK, ARE YOU?

NOT NOW, BUT MAYBE LATER. TONS OF PEOPLE GET SICK BECAUSE THEY DON'T BUY MEDICINE IN TIME...I'D LIKE TO BUY A GALLON OF MEDICINE.
WHAT KIND OF MEDICINE?

HMM. THE KIND OF MEDICINE FOR WHOOPING COUGH AND BLISTERS AND STOMACHACHES AND FOR IF YOU GET A PEA STUCK IN YOUR NOSE. AND IT WOULD BE GOOD IF I COULD USE IT TO POLISH FURNITURE TOO.

EXCUSE ME, MY DEAR PHARMACYIST, WHAT'S BEST FOR A STOMACHACHE—EATING A WARM DUMPLING OR SOAKING YOUR STOMACH IN COLD WATER?
GET OUT!

BOY, HE SURE WAS ANGRY! YOU'D THINK I'D DONE SOMETHING WRONG. I'M GOING TO TRY A WARM DUMPLING, AND HE WILL HAVE HIMSELF TO BLAME IF IT DOESN'T WORK.

PIPPI GOES ON A PICNIC
I LOVE GOING ON PICNICS.
WHAT A DUMB COW. IT WON'T MOVE OUT OF THE WAY.
I KNOW. COWS CAN BE SO BULLHEADED.
OOH! I HOPE THERE AREN'T ANY BULLS IN THIS PASTURE.
AND WHAT HAPPENS? THEN THE BULLS GET COWHEADED, OF COURSE.

GREAT! WHAT'S IN THE BASKET, PIPPI?
WE'LL SIT UP THERE ON THAT ROCK AND EAT OUR LUNCH.

OH, THIS IS SO GOOD!
CAN I HAVE ANOTHER PANCAKE?

BE CAREFUL, PIPPI! DON'T FALL OFF!
I'M NOT GOING TO FALL, I'M GOING TO FLY.

WELL, THAT DIDN'T WORK. I GUESS I HAD TOO MANY PANCAKES IN MY STOMACH.

IN THE MEANTIME, MR. NILSSON HAS GONE OFF ON HIS OWN LITTLE EXPEDITION.

STUPID MR. NILSSON! HE ONCE RAN AWAY IN SURABAYA AND TOOK A JOB AS A SERVANT FOR AN OLD WIDOW.

A BULL!
HELP, PIPPI!

EXCUSE ME FOR INTERRUPTING.

THIS IS HOW THEY DO IT IN SPAIN.

BUT THIS IS HOW I DO IT.
AND SOMETIMES LIKE THIS.

PIPPI HATES CRUELTY TO ANIMALS
OH, LOOK, HE'S HITTING THAT POOR HORSE!
HELLO THERE! WHOSE NAUGHTY LITTLE BOY ARE YOU?
AND WHY ARE YOU HITTING THAT HORSE?
IT'S NONE OF YOUR BUSINESS, SO KEEP OUT OF IT, OR ELSE I MIGHT BEAT YOU TOO.

THAT WON'T HAPPEN, 'CAUSE YOUR STICK IS BROKEN.

COMPLETELY BROKEN! AND IF YOU DON'T WATCH OUT...

YOU MIGHT BREAK INTO PIECES TOO!
HELP!
HELP!

HA HA! HE DIDN'T KNOW HOW STRONG PIPPI IS!

DON'T EVER HIT YOUR HORSE AGAIN! OKAY?
OR THERE'LL BE TROUBLE!
AND, BY THE WAY, I THINK YOU CAN CARRY YOUR OWN SACKS HOME FOR A CHANGE.

ALSO, I'LL CARRY YOUR HORSE FOR A CHANGE.
HE LOOKS LIKE HE COULD USE A LITTLE REST.
I'M SORRY, LITTLE GIRL. I'LL NEVER BE MEAN TO MY HORSE AGAIN.
GOOD. EVERYONE SHOULD BE NICE TO ANIMALS...
AND CARRY THEM WHEN THEY GET TIRED.

PIPPI GOES TO THE FAIR

WOW, THOSE TWO SNAKES ARE REALLY SCARY!
ULF + LISA
BOA CONSTRICT

WHAT A BIG BOA CONSTRICTOR... SHE'S SO BRAVE!

I WONDER WHETHER THE OTHER ONE IS A BOA TOO...

LITTLE GIRL, HE'LL CRUSH YOU TO DEATH!
HE WON'T CRUSH ME. I DON'T FALL FOR OLD TRICKS LIKE THAT. BELIEVE ME...

OVER IN INDIA I SAW WAY BIGGER SNAKES THAN THIS.

YOU'RE REALLY NOT SCARED OF SNAKES?
NOPE. NICE LITTLE SNAKES LIKE THIS DON'T SCARE ME. SLEEP TIGHT, LITTLE FRIEND!

HERE COMES PIPPI LONGSTOCKING!

IF YOU BITE ME, I'LL BITE YOU RIGHT BACK!

NOW YOU HAD BETTER CALM DOWN!
PIPPI, HE TORE YOUR DRESS.

JUST HOLD ON A SECOND AND I'LL EVEN IT OUT. THEN I'LL BE A FANCY LADY AGAIN.
BUT SHOULD A FANCY LADY'S STOMACH BE GROWLING?

PIPPI IS SHIPWRECKED

BEFORE PIPPI MOVED INTO VILLA VILLEKULLA, SHE SAILED THE SEAS WITH HER FATHER, CAPTAIN LONGSTOCKING, ON THE SHIP HOPPETOSSA. BUT, ONE DAY, PIPPI'S FATHER WAS BLOWN OVERBOARD AND DISAPPEARED.

HERE COMES THE SHIPWRECK!
EVERY MAN FOR HIMSELF!

BUT JUST STAY IN THE BOAT SO YOU WON'T GET YOUR FEET WET.

WHAT WAS THAT?
IT SOUNDED LIKE A SNARLING CANNIBAL!

ONE MORE SNARL AND THERE'S GOING TO BE TROUBLE. I DIDN'T COME HERE TO HAVE SOME CANNIBAL COOK ME UP WITH STEWED CARROTS. I HATE CARROTS.
OOH, PIPPI, DON'T SAY THAT!
HA, THERE AREN'T ANY CANNIBALS HERE.
WHAT, YOU DON'T LIKE CAR-ROTS, EITHER?

WHAT A GREAT TENT WE HAVE, AND SUCH A NICE CAMPFIRE.
YES, IT'S GOOD TO HAVE A FIRE. IT KEEPS THE WILD ANIMALS AWAY.

OH, YOU'RE SCARING ME! WHAT WILD ANIMALS?
MOSQUITOES.

YUMMY SANDWICHES! I LIKE THE ONES WITH HAM BEST.

MY FAVORITE ARE THE ONES WITH MEATBALLS.

MY FAVORITE ARE THE ONES WITH HAM AND MEATBALLS AND LIVERWURST AND CHEESE.

TIME FOR BED. BUT YOU NEED TO SLEEP HERE, MY HORSIE. IT'S TOO CROWDED FOR YOU INSIDE THE TENT.

PiPPi is STiLL SHiP-WRECKED
IT'S SO MUCH FUN BEING SHIPWRECKED ON THIS DESERT ISLAND!
YEAH, BUT TODAY WE NEED TO GO BACK HOME. OTHERWISE MAMMA WILL WORRY.
ARE YOU FISHING, PIPPI?
NO, IT JUST LOOKS LIKE I AM.
WHAT ARE YOU FISHING FOR?
OCTOPUS. BUT ONLY THE PERCH ARE BITING. COME ON, LET'S GO SWIMMING INSTEAD!

I FOUND THIS GREAT SLED! WE CAN USE IT TO SLIDE INTO THE WATER.
WAIT, PIPPI, WHERE'S THE BOAT?
IT'S GONE! HOW ARE WE GOING TO GET HOME?
OHHHH, I WANT TO GO HOME TO MAMMA!
HOME? WE'RE GOING TO STAY HERE FOR AT LEAST SEVEN YEARS.

OKAY, LET'S SEND OFF A MESSAGE IN A BOTTLE SO WE'LL GET RESCUED. TOMMY, YOU CAN WRITE IT.
HERE'S WHAT TO WRITE: "HELP US BEFORE WE PERISH. WE'VE BEEN PINING AWAY FOR TWO DAYS ON THIS ISLAND WITHOUT ANY SNUFF."
I CAN'T WRITE THAT.
WHY NOT? WE DON'T HAVE ANY SNUFF, DO WE?
NO, BUT WE DON'T USE SNUFF.
EXACTLY. THAT'S WHY WE DON'T HAVE ANY. JUST WRITE WHAT I SAID.

OKAY, COME AND RESCUE US!

DO PEOPLE THINK WE DON'T HAVE ANYTHING BETTER TO DO THAN SIT AND WAIT TO BE RESCUED? WHAT'S KEEPING THEM?

WAIT A MINUTE. I JUST REMEMBERED SOMETHING. I CARRIED THE BOAT UP ON LAND LAST NIGHT.
WHY'D YOU DO THAT?
SO IT WOULDN'T GET WET.

WE'RE RESCUING OURSELVES! I'D LIKE TO SEE THEM TRY TO RESCUE US NOW; IT'D SERVE THEM RIGHT.

PIPPI LONGSTOCKING
Gets into a Fight
THIS IS HOW I SCRUB THE FLOOR.
YOU'RE SO SMART, PIPPI!

OH, LISTEN TO THEM FIGHTING OUTSIDE!
THEY'RE REALLY GOING AT IT.
I SHOULD HAVE BEEN AN ICE-SKATING STAR.
IT'S THAT HORRIBLE BENGT. HE'S ALWAYS FIGHTING.
IS IT A PRIVATE FIGHT, OR CAN ANYBODY JOIN IN?

NOW WE'RE REALLY GOING TO LET YOU HAVE IT!

THE BOYS DIDN'T KNOW THAT PIPPI IS THE STRONGEST IN THE WORLD.

LIKE I SAID, YOU DON'T KNOW HOW TO TREAT A LADY.

THAT'S WHERE YOU CAN STAY UNTIL YOU GROW UP AND LEARN SOME SENSE.

AND YOU CAN SIT UP THERE UNTIL YOUR MAMMA COMES TO GET YOU DOWN.

A LITTLE RIDE NEVER HURTS.

OR A LITTLE FLYING THROUGH THE AIR.
HA, HA, PIPPI'S THE STRONGEST IN THE WORLD.

DID YOU SAY YOU
WANTED TO FLY TOO?

IF THERE'S
ANYTHING ELSE
YOU'D LIKE TO
SAY ABOUT
MY HAIR OR
MY SHOES...
TELL ME
NOW BEFORE
I GO HOME.

DON'T CRY
ANYMORE,
VILLY.
IF THEY BOTHER
YOU AGAIN, JUST
TELL PIPPI.

PIPPI, WHY EXACTLY
ARE YOUR SHOES
SO BIG?
SO I CAN WIGGLE MY
TOES, OF COURSE.

Pippi and the Burglars

ON A DARK AUTUMN NIGHT TWO SHABBY-LOOKING BURGLARS CAME TRUDGING DOWN THE ROAD OUTSIDE VILLA VILLEKULLA WHERE PIPPI LIVED.

PIPPI HAD A WHOLE SUITCASE FULL OF GOLD COINS THAT HER FATHER HAD GIVEN HER.

THE BURGLARS DIDN'T KNOW THAT MR. NILSSON WAS PIPPI'S LITTLE MONKEY, WHO WAS ASLEEP IN HIS LITTLE DOLL BED.

THAT'S MR. NILSSON TO YOU. AND HE'S SLEEPING IN THE LITTLE GREEN DOLL BED.

YOU DON'T MIND IF WE TAKE THIS MONEY, DO YOU?
OF COURSE NOT.

AND YOU DON'T MIND IF I TAKE IT BACK, DO YOU?

WATCH IT, KID!

TIDDLY-POM AND PIDDLY-DEE.

DEAR SWEET GIRL, PLEASE FORGIVE US. WE WERE JUST JOKING.
STAY UP THERE AND TAKE A REST.

CAN YOU DANCE THE POLKA? I CAN.

OH, IT'S SO FUN TO DANCE. I JUST LEARNED HOW, YOU KNOW. BUT NOW LET'S HAVE SOME FOOD.
WE'RE REALLY HUNGRY.

THIS IS YUMMY.
I THINK I NEED TO POUR A LITTLE MILK IN MY EAR. THAT'S GOOD FOR AN EARACHE.
POOR THING. DO YOU HAVE AN EARACHE?

NO, BUT MAYBE I WILL SOMEDAY.

PIPPI IS INVITED FOR COFFEE
PIPPI, DO YOU WANT TO HAVE COFFEE WITH US? SOME LADIES ARE COMING OVER TOO.
COFFEE? OH, I'M SO NERVOUS. WHAT IF I CAN'T BEHAVE?
I'M SURE YOU CAN! COME OVER TOMORROW.
TO ARMS!
COMPANY–FORWARD, MARCH!
GOODNESS GRACIOUS, WHO IS THAT?

ARMS, FORWARD. KNEES, BEND! I'M A LITTLE SHY, YOU SEE, SO I NEED TO ISSUE ORDERS.

LITTLE CHILDREN SHOULD BE SEEN AND NOT HEARD.
WHY'S THAT? THE EARS NEED A LITTLE EXERCISE, TOO. THEY'RE NOT JUST FOR WIGGLING, ARE THEY?

OH, WHAT CHARMING LADIES!

PIPPI, COME AND SIT OVER HERE SO WE CAN SHOW YOU THE ALBUM.
SURE, BUT FIRST I NEED SOMETHING IN MY BELLY.

DIDN'T YOU EVER LEARN THAT CHILDREN ARE SERVED LAST?
WOW, THAT LOOKS GOOD. WHEN DO WE START?
SURE, BUT I ALWAYS THINK...

THAT IT'S BEST TO DIG IN WHILE THERE ARE STILL SOME COOKIES LEFT. THOSE LADIES SURE LOOK HUNGRY!

PLEASE HELP YOURSELVES TO SOME CAKE WHILE I GET MORE COFFEE.
NO USE LOOKING LIKE A SOUR PICKLE WHEN YOU'RE INVITED TO COFFEE.

WHAT A SPLENDID CREAM CAKE. AND A LOVELY LITTLE CANDY IN THE MIDDLE!

I'M TAKING IT!
NO, NO, PIPPI!

WHAT A HORRID CHILD!

NO USE GETTING UPSET ABOUT SUCH A LITTLE MISHAP. THE IMPORTANT THING IS TO STAY HEALTHY.

WANT A BITE?

I KNEW IT. I TRIED BUT I COULDN'T BEHAVE MYSELF. I'M SORRY.

YOU NAUGHTY CHILD. YOU CAN'T COME OVER TO PLAY WITH TOMMY AND ANNIKA ANYMORE.

DON'T BE SAD, PIPPI. YOU'LL BEHAVE BETTER NEXT TIME.

YOU THINK SO? I COULD GET UP AN HOUR EARLIER IN THE MORNING AND PRACTICE.

PIPPI AND THE FIRE
COME ON, MR. NILSSON. WE'RE GOING FOR A LITTLE RIDE.

WHERE'S THAT SMOKE COMING FROM?

FIRE! FIRE!

WHAT A BLAZE!

WE CAN'T GET OUT! SOMEBODY SET FIRE TO THE STAIRS!
STAY CALM. WE'LL BRING YOU DOWN ON THE LADDER.

IT'S NO USE. THE LADDER'S TOO SHORT.
POOR KIDS. THEY'RE GOING TO BURN UP!

I REFUSE TO BELIEVE THAT.

WE CAN FIX THINGS IF WE'RE CLEVER.

TIE THE ROPE UP THERE, MR. NILSSON.

PIPPI FIXES EVERYTHING.

YOU LOOK SO SAD. HAVE YOU GOT A TUMMY ACHE?

THIS IS ALMOST LIKE WALKING A TIGHTROPE.

HERE COMES THE LITTLE DUMPLING.

HERE'S THE OTHER ONE.
HURRAY, PIPPI LONGSTOCKING!

YOU SAVED THOSE KIDS. WE'LL GIVE YOU ANYTHING YOU WANT.

GREAT! THEN I WANT TO SPRAY YOU WITH THE FIRE HOSE.
GLUG, GLUG!
THAT WAS FUN. DON'T YOU THINK SO?

PIPPI HAS A BIRTH-DAY
DON'T BE SO NOSY, MR. NILSSON. I'M WRITING TO TOMMY AND ANNIKA.
TMMY & ANIKA kOm TO piPPis BertDAY PaRtee TOmorow AfturNoon
A BIRTHDAY PARTY. HOW NICE! WHAT KIND OF PRESENT SHOULD WE BUY?
PIPPI WILL BE SO HAPPY!
WE WISH YOU A HAPPY BIRTHDAY!
A MUSIC BOX. JUST WHAT I'VE ALWAYS WANTED.

I'VE NEVER BEEN TO A BIRTHDAY PARTY WITH A HORSE BEFORE.

DON'T TOUCH THE FLOOR–IT'S A GREAT GAME. YOU CAN'T STEP ON THE FLOOR, ONLY THE FURNITURE.

TIDDLY-POM AND PIDDLY-DEE.
SUGAR
SALT
COFFEE

BUT WE COULD ALSO GO UP IN THE ATTIC AND VISIT THE GHOSTS.

ARE THERE G-G-GHOSTS IN THE ATTIC?
TONS OF THEM. IT'S SWARMING WITH GHOSTS. I LOVE GHOSTS!
SUGAR
SALT
COFFEE

HI, ALL YOU GHOSTS AND SPOOKS!
OH, PIPPI, I'M SO SCARED!
MAMMA SAYS THERE'S NO SUCH THING AS A GHOST.

WRONG! THE MORE I THINK ABOUT IT, THE MORE IT WAS JUST

OKAY, THERE'S PAPPA'S OLD SEA CHEST.

WHAT'S IN IT?
HOW EXCITING! OPEN IT!
A SACK OF GOLD COINS AND TWO PIRATE PISTOLS AND PAPPA'S OLD NIGHTSHIRT.

PIPPI, YOU ALMOST LOOK LIKE A GHOST. OH, I'M SO SCARED!
NIGHTSHIRTS AREN'T DANGEROUS. THEY ONLY BITE IN SELF-DEFENSE.

BANG!
BANG!
JUST THINK, I MIGHT HAVE HIT A GHOST IN THE LEG. IT SERVES THEM RIGHT EVEN IF THEY DON'T EXIST. THERE'S NO NEED FOR THEM TO GO AROUND SCARING LITTLE KIDS OUT OF THEIR WITS.

I'M GOING TO BE A PIRATE WHEN I GROW UP. HOW ABOUT YOU?

PIPPI'S CHRISTMAS TREE PARTY
HEY, LISTEN TO THE WIND WHISTLING.

LOOK, SHE'S MADE A SKI SLOPE ON THE ROOF.
DO YOU WANT TO COME TO MY CHRISTMAS TREE PARTY TONIGHT?
SURE!

EXCEPT I DON'T HAVE A CHRISTMAS TREE. DO I NEED ONE?
OF COURSE YOU DO!

WILL THIS ONE DO?
BUT THERE AREN'T ANY CANDIES OR LIGHTS OR FLAGS ON IT.

BUT WHEN NIGHT FELL, PIPPI'S TREE LOOKED LIKE THIS.
OH, PIPPI, IT'S WONDERFUL!
LOOK!

OKAY, LET'S GO INTO MY IGLOO. AN IGLOO IS ONE OF THE BEST PLACES FOR A CHRISTMAS TREE PARTY.

AND CHOCOLATE AND CREAM CAKE ARE SOME OF THE BEST THINGS TO EAT AT A CHRISTMAS TREE PARTY.

LOOK, THEY'RE EATING CREAM CAKE!
WE WANT SOME CREAM CAKE TOO. OTHERWISE WE'LL BEAT YOU UP. DO YOU HEAR ME?

WE HEAR YOU LOUD AND CLEAR. WAS IT CREAM CAKE YOU WANTED?
YES.
OTHERWISE WE'LL WRECK YOUR HUT. SO HAND OVER THAT CREAM CAKE RIGHT NOW!

YOU'RE IN A HURRY? OKAY, IN THAT CASE...

DON'T WORRY, TOMMY AND ANNIKA. WE HAVE MORE CAKES.
AFTERWARD WE'LL GO SLEDDING OFF THE ROOF.

OUT OF THE WAY! HERE COME THE SWEDES!

NOW I THINK IT'S TIME TO PLUNDER THE CHRISTMAS TREE.

I LIKE CLIMBING IN CHRISTMAS TREES.
LOOK FOR YOUR PACKAGES. THERE ARE PRESENTS INSIDE.

I WONDER WHAT'S IN THIS PACKAGE.
TOMMY
ANNIKA
OPEN IT AND LET'S SEE.

OH!
LOOK, A DOLL!
A CAR! YOU'RE SO NICE, PIPPI!
YOU'RE WELCOME. BUT LISTEN, SHOULDN'T WE DANCE AROUND THE CHRISTMAS TREE?

COME ON, LET'S SING A LIVELY TUNE! THE ONE ABOUT "THE FRISKY FOX FLIES THROUGH THE FIELDS TILL EASTER." A PERFECT SONG FOR PLUNDERING THE CHRISTMAS TREE!

Pippi Wel-comes a Visi-tor
PIPPI, ARE YOU GOING TO KEEP LIVING HERE IN VILLA VILLEKULLA? I MEAN, UNTIL YOU GROW UP AND BECOME A PIRATE?
YOU NEVER KNOW. ONE FINE DAY, MY FATHER MIGHT COME AND GET ME.
BUT DO YOU THINK HE'S REALLY ALIVE?
OF COURSE HE'S ALIVE. I CAN SEE HIM MOVING. REALLY.
HERE HE COMES NOW.
YOU'VE GROWN SO BIG, PAPPA EPHRAIM!
PIPPILOTTA, MY BELOVED CHILD. I WAS GOING TO SAY HOW BIG YOU'VE GROWN.

I KNOW, THAT'S WHY
I SAID IT FIRST.
SEEMS LIKE YOU ARE AS STRONG AS EVER, PIPPI!

STRONGER. SHALL WE ARM-WRESTLE?

HURRAY! PIPPI IS THE STRONGEST IN THE WORLD.

WHO ARE THESE NICE LITTLE KIDS?
THAT'S TOMMY AND ANNIKA.

IS IT TRUE THAT YOU'RE REALLY A KING?

OF COURSE. I'M KING OF THE KURRAKURRADOOTAS ON KURRAKURRADOOT ISLAND.

HURRAY! THAT MEANS I'M A PRINCESS!

THIS IS HOW I LOOK WHEN I'M RULING. KING EPHRAIM LONGSTOCKING I.

GREAT, HUH? COME ON, PIPPI, LET'S DANCE.

WATCH OUT AND DON'T BREAK THE FLOOR.
YAY, LET'S SPIN AND TWIRL.
THEIR DANCE IS SO WILD. IT ALMOST SCARES ME.
YIKES! HE FELL IN THE FIREWOOD BIN.
ARRGH! THIS IS SO MUCH FUN.
ARE YOU STUCK? ARE YOU TOO FAT, PAPPA?
DON'T T-T-TICKLE MY FEET. I'M GOING TO DIE LAUGHING.
I THINK THAT GRASS SKIRT NEEDS SOME EXPERT MENDING.
I KNOW. BUT WE'VE SURE HAD SOME FUN.

Pippi Has Strong Teeth!
LOOK, THERE'S MY BOAT.
DEAR OLD HOPPETOSSA! LET'S GO ON BOARD.
HI, FRIDOLF. WHAT'S THE MATTER WITH YOU?
TOOTHACHE.
HAVE YOU BEEN BUYING MORE CANDY?
CANDY IS SO GOOD.
BUT TOOTHACHES AREN'T SO GOOD. BRING THE CANDY HERE AND WE'LL TOSS IT INTO THE SEA.

HOW CAN YOU SAY THAT WHEN YOU SOMETIMES BUY THIRTY POUNDS OF CANDY?
DON'T BE SILLY! I ONLY EAT CANDY ONCE A YEAR. BUT YOU MUNCH ON IT EVERY DAY.

IT'S THANKS TO HARDTACK AND CARROTS THAT I HAVE TEETH LIKE THIS.

AND LIKE THIS! BUT I HAVEN'T EATEN CANDY SINCE THE SPRING OF 1914.
OW, IT HURTS SO BAD I THINK MY HEAD'S GOING TO SPLIT.

LOOK WHAT MY DAUGHTER CAN DO! THAT'S WHAT I CALL STRONG TEETH.

YOUR TEETH ARE SUPER STRONG TOO. SHALL WE FIND OUT WHOSE ARE THE STRONGEST?

COME ON, PIPPI!
COME ON, PIPPI!

YOU WIN, PIPPI! I THINK I NEED TO EAT SOME MORE HARDTACK.

WE'RE GOING TO STOP EATING CANDY TOO.
WE WANT TO HAVE STRONG TEETH LIKE PIPPI.

GRANDMA HAD REALLY STRONG TEETH. IF YOU STUCK A NAIL IN HER MOUTH...
SHE WOULD BITE IT OFF.

I BET YOUR GRANDMA NEVER ATE CANDY.
NO, SHE ATE ONLY NAILS. AND SHE HAD TEETH LIKE A LION.

PiPPi GiVeS a FaReWell PARTY
ARE YOU REALLY GOING WITH YOUR FATHER TO THE SOUTH SEAS, PIPPI?
OF COURSE! PRINCESS— THAT'S NOT A BAD JOB FOR SOMEONE WITH NO SCHOOLING, LIKE ME.

BUT FIRST I'M GIVING A FAREWELL PARTY. DO YOU THINK TWENTY CAKES ARE ENOUGH?

IF THERE'S GOING TO BE A PARTY, I'D BETTER WEAR MY ROYAL FINERY.

HERE COME MY SAILORS. HI, FRIDOLF!
HI, YOUR MAJESTY.

WE WANT TO COME TOO.
THANKS FOR COMING. WELCOME!

LOOK, A KURRAKURRADOOT KING!

DOES EVERYONE HAVE SAUSAGE?

THANKS! HIS MAJESTY AND I HAVE PLENTY.
AND NOW WE'LL HAVE CAKE.

AND THEN WE'LL PLAY FOLLOW THE LEADER. CAN EVERYBODY DO THIS?

EVERYONE UP ON THE ROOF!

KOOKELIKOO!

YOUR MAJESTY, WON'T YOU COME DOWN AND COMPETE WITH PIPPI? WE WANT TO SEE WHO'S THE STRONGEST.

HURRAY! PIPPI IS THE STRONGEST IN THE WORLD.

Pippi goes on board
WHAT A NICE HOUSE THIS IS. NO FLEAS, AND GRAND IN EVERY WAY. I'M ALMOST SORRY I HAVE TO LEAVE.

WHEN DOES THE BOAT LEAVE, PIPPI?
I THINK IT LEAVES AS SOON AS I GO ON BOARD.

HEY, PIPPI. HURRY UP AND COME ON BOARD SO WE CAN SET SAIL.

READ THE POEM WE WROTE FOR PIPPI.
I CAN'T. IT'LL MAKE ME CRY.

YOU'RE ALREADY CRYING. SO I'D BETTER READ IT MYSELF.

GOODBYE, DEAR PIPPI, YOUR TIME WITH US NOW ENDS, BUT WE WILL FOREVER BE YOUR LOYAL FRIENDS.

DON'T CRY, ANNIKA. IT MAKES ME SAD.

IT'S OKAY, HORSEY. DON'T BE SCARED. JUST LOOK AT MR. NILSSON. HE'S AS COOL AS A CUCUMBER.

BYE, TOMMY. BYE, ANNIKA. DON'T FORGET ME!
NO, WE'LL NEVER FORGET YOU, PIPPI!

WELCOME, PIPPI! PULL UP THE GANGPLANK, FRIDOLF.
NO, PAPPA, I CAN'T DO THIS. I CAN'T LEAVE TOMMY AND ANNIKA.
ARE YOU SURE? WELL, YOU DO HAVE A MORE ORDERLY LIFE IN VILLA VILLEKULLA.

AN ORDERLY LIFE IS THE BEST THING FOR KIDS. ESPECIALLY IF THEY CAN ARRANGE IT THEMSELVES.

YOU'RE...YOU'RE NOT ON THE BOAT?
THREE GUESSES!

WAIT, PIPPI. HERE ARE SOME MORE GOLD COINS.
PLOP!

THANKS, PAPPA EPHRAIM! NOW I'M AS RICH AS A TROLL AGAIN.

LET'S RIDE HOME TO VILLA VILLEKULLA!
OH, PIPPI, IT'S SO NICE OF YOU TO STAY HERE WITH US.

Pippi finds a Spoonk
JUST THINK, I'VE FOUND A NEW WORD. AN EXCELLENT WORD: SPOONK.
SPOONK? WHAT DOES IT MEAN?

I DON'T KNOW, AND THAT BOTHERS ME. BUT MAYBE WE CAN BUY A SPOONK IN THE STORE.
SHALL WE GO AND ASK?

I'D LIKE TO BUY A BAG OF SPOONK. BUT IT HAS TO BE FRESH.
I'M AFRAID WE'RE OUT OF SPOONK TODAY.

OH, DID YOU HAVE ANY SPOONK YESTERDAY? DID IT HAVE RED STRIPES?
ACTUALLY, I HAVE NO IDEA WHAT SPOONK IS.
KOLA

I'D LIKE TO BUY A SPOONK. BUT IT HAS TO BE TOP-NOTCH, THE KIND FOR KILLING LIONS.

WILL THIS DO?
THAT'S WHAT THE PROFESSORS CALL A RAKE BUT A SPOONK IS WHAT I WANT.

MAYBE IT TURNS OUT THAT SPOONK IS AN ILLNESS. COME ON, LET'S ASK THE DOCTOR.
DR. KVAX
DAILY 1-2
RING 3X

SO WHAT'S WRONG WITH YOU?
I'M AFRAID THAT I'VE COME DOWN WITH SPOONK. I ITCH ALL OVER, AND I CAN'T KEEP MY EYES OPEN WHEN I SLEEP. SOMETIMES I HICCUP.

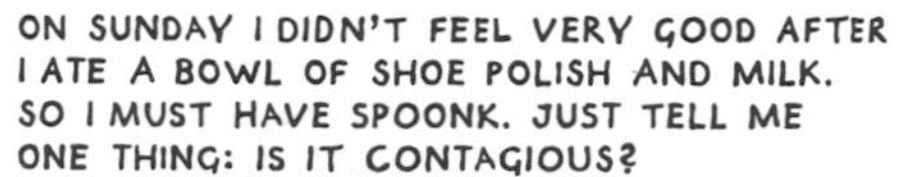
ON SUNDAY I DIDN'T FEEL VERY GOOD AFTER I ATE A BOWL OF SHOE POLISH AND MILK. SO I MUST HAVE SPOONK. JUST TELL ME ONE THING: IS IT CONTAGIOUS?

A
BCFI
XPYTL
JKMOR
NHUOAFDS

I THINK YOU'RE HEALTHIER THAN MOST PEOPLE. BESIDES, THERE'S NO ILLNESS CALLED SPOONK.

MAYBE THERE'S A SPOONK IN THERE. I'LL CLIMB UP AND TAKE A LOOK.

CAN YOU TELL ME IF THERE'S A SPOONK IN HERE?

OH, SOMETHING'S GOTTEN LOOSE! IS HE DANGEROUS? DOES HE BITE?
I THINK HE DOES. LOOK AND SEE IF HE'S UNDER THE BED.

THERE'S NOT EVEN A WHISKER OF A SPOONK IN HERE. BYE!

STOP! DON'T STEP ON THAT BEETLE, TOMMY!

WHAT A PRETTY LITTLE THING. I WONDER WHAT KIND IT IS.
IT'S A SPOONK.
ARE YOU SURE?

DON'T YOU THINK I KNOW A SPOONK WHEN I SEE ONE? MY SWEET LITTLE SPOONK, WE'VE BEEN RUNNING ALL OVER TOWN LOOKING FOR YOU, AND YOU WERE RIGHT OUTSIDE VILLA VILLEKULLA THE WHOLE TIME.

Pippi's Christmas Guests
PIPPI, WE'RE GOING TO GRANDMA'S HOUSE FOR CHRISTMAS.
POOR PIPPI. WHAT ARE YOU GOING TO DO ON CHRISTMAS EVE ALL ALONE?

I'M GOING TO DANCE AROUND THE TREE WITH MY HORSE AND MR. NILSSON.
GOODBYE, DEAR, DEAR, PIPPI. MERRY CHRISTMAS!

TIDDLY-POM AND PIDDLY-DEE. THE WHOLE HOUSE WILL BE SNOWED IN WHEN YOU GET BACK.

WELL, IT LOOKS LIKE SOMEONE WANTS TO COME IN.
WOOF, WOOF!

YOU'RE RIGHT, THIS IS NO WEATHER FOR A DOG.

OR FOR A CAT
EITHER, IT SEEMS.

PRETTY SOON WE CAN OPEN
OUR OWN ZOO. WAIT, I HEAR
A LITTLE BIRD CHEEPING!

YOU SAY YOU DON'T LIKE SNOWSTORMS?
YOU SAY YOU'D LIKE A CHRISTMAS BUN?

MR. NILSSON GETS BANANAS, AND THE HORSE GETS OATS.

LITTLE PIPPI GETS A LITTLE CHRISTMAS BUN, AND BIG PIPPI GETS A BIG CHRISTMAS BUN. FAIR'S FAIR.

AND EVERYONE CAN HAVE APPLES AND GINGERSNAPS FROM THE TREE.

AND I'LL BE SANTA CLAUS. DO YOU THINK THIS WILL MAKE A GOOD BEARD?

MERRY CHRISTMAS TO ALL OF US!

??? PIPPI PLAYS THE GUESSING GAME ???
PIPPI, COME WITH US TO SCHOOL TODAY.
MISS ROSENBLOM IS COMING, AND I'M SO SCARED.
ONCE IN A WHILE A STERN, OLD WOMAN COMES TO TOMMY AND ANNIKA'S SCHOOL TO QUESTION THE CHILDREN. THOSE WHO ANSWER CORRECTLY WIN SOCKS AND UNDERWEAR. THE OTHERS HAVE TO STAND IN THE CORNER.

BUT WHY? DOES SHE BITE?
NO, BUT SHE ASKS SO MANY QUESTIONS. AND IF YOU WEIGH LESS THAN FIFTY-FIVE POUNDS, YOU HAVE TO GO HOME WITH HER AND EAT SLIMY SOUP.

LET'S MAKE TWO LINES, CHILDREN. IF YOU HAVE LITTLE BROTHERS AND SISTERS, STAND ON THE LEFT. IF YOU DON'T HAVE ANY, STAND ON THE RIGHT.

WHERE DO I STAND IF I DON'T HAVE FOURTEEN BROTHERS AND SISTERS, INCLUDING ELEVEN NAUGHTY LITTLE BOYS?

IN THE CORNER YOU GO. BUT FIRST LET ME WEIGH YOU.
COULD YOU ALSO MEASURE MY CHEST AND MY HEIGHT ABOVE SEA LEVEL?
NO SOUP FOR YOU.
SOMETIMES I GET LUCKY. NOW I NEED TO MAKE SURE I DON'T WIN ANY UNDERSHIRTS.
10.00
PLEASE TELL ME HOW YOU'D SPELL "SEASICK."
I'D LOVE TO. S-E-E-S-I-K.
WELL, THAT'S NOT HOW IT'S SPELLED IN THE DICTIONARY.
THEN IT'S A GOOD THING YOU ASKED ME HOW I SPELL IT.

TOMMY, CAN YOU TELL ME HOW MANY INCHES ARE IN A YARD?
THIRTY-SIX.
THAT'S WHAT YOU THINK! IN BAD YEARS THERE ARE ONLY TWENTY.
PER AND PAL ARE SHARING A CAKE. IF PER GETS ONE-FOURTH, WHAT DOES PAL GET?
A STOMACHACHE.
WHEN DID KING KARL XII DIE?
WHAT! HE'S DEAD? I DIDN'T EVEN KNOW HE WAS SICK.
GO STAND IN THE CORNER RIGHT NOW.
THAT'S NOT FAIR! I ANSWERED ALL YOUR QUESTIONS.

LET'S PLAY OUR OWN GUESSING GAME. TELL ME THE NAME OF SOMEONE WHO'S DEAD.
KARL XII.

WHAT CLEVER KIDS! EVERYBODY WHO KNOWS THAT KARL XII IS DEAD GETS A GOLD COIN.

AND EVERYBODY WHO WEIGHS AT LEAST SIX POUNDS GETS FREE ICE CREAM ALL DAY LONG.

HOW NICE OF YOU, PIPPI, TO GIVE US ICE CREAM AND GOLD COINS.
AND I'VE SPARED YOU FROM SCRATCHY WOOLEN UNDERWEAR TOO.

PIPPI REFUSES TO SELL HER HOUSE
I WONDER IF THIS IS THE OLD SHACK THAT'S FOR SALE. IT SHOULD BE CHEAP.
ONE DAY, A RICH AND VERY STUPID MAN SHOWED UP. HE WANTED TO BUY PIPPI'S HOUSE.

NICE PIECE OF LAND. WE COULD JUST TEAR DOWN THE HOUSE.
SURE, LET'S GET STARTED.

AND WE COULD CHOP DOWN THAT TREE.
OH NO, DON'T DO THAT. IT'S SUCH A GOOD CLIMBING TREE.

DO I LOOK LIKE I WANT TO CLIMB TREES?
NO, BUT WE DO! AND BESIDES, IT'S A LEMONADE TREE.

WHAT NONSENSE! I DON'T WANT ANY KIDS AROUND HERE. THEY'RE SUCH PESTS.
I AGREE. ALL KIDS SHOULD BE SHOT.

BUT THEN NOBODY WOULD GROW UP TO BE NICE, BIG MEN—AND WE CAN'T LET THAT HAPPEN.

SOUNDS LIKE YOU'RE TRYING TO BE FUNNY. WHAT'S YOUR NAME?
MY NAME IS PIPPI LONGSTOCKING. IF YOU NEED TO TEAR DOWN A HOUSE OR ANYTHING ELSE, I CAN HELP. JUST LET ME KNOW.

SILLY GIRL. CAN YOU TELL ME WHO OWNS THIS HOUSE?
THE OWNER IS A LITTLE BUSY RIGHT NOW.

LOOK AT WHAT RED HAIR YOU HAVE. DO YOU KNOW WHY YOU LOOK LIKE A LIT MATCH?
NO, BUT I'VE AL-WAYS WONDERED ABOUT THAT.

YOU BOTH HAVE A FIERY TOP. HA, HA!

HA, HA! BUT DID YOU KNOW THAT YOU'RE JUST LIKE ME?

I HOPE NOT.
IT'S TRUE! WE'VE BOTH GOT A BIG MOUTH...EXCEPT I DON'T.

ARE YOU BEING RUDE? I'LL GIVE YOU SOMETHING ELSE TO THINK ABOUT.

LIKE WHAT?
I'LL WAIT FOR YOU TO COME DOWN. THEN I'LL GIVE YOU A SPANKING.

I'M NOT COMING DOWN UNTIL NOVEMBER.
HA, HA!

MAYBE YOU NEED A SPANKING TOO.

I DON'T HAVE TIME FOR THIS ANYMORE. ONE DAY A WEEK I TEAR DOWN HOUSES. BUT NOT ON FRIDAYS, BECAUSE THAT'S MY CLEANING DAY.

Pippi cheers up Aunt Laura
AUNT LAURA IS SOMEBODY I'D LIKE TO MEET.
ARE YOU SURE YOU KNOW HOW TO TALK TO AUNTS?

YOU JUST CHEER THEM UP. THAT'S WHAT I'LL DO WITH AUNT LAURA.

HI GUYS! COULD I HAVE A LITTLE JUICE SO MY THROAT WON'T GET DRY ONCE WE START TALKING?

YOU NEED TO KEEP QUIET, PIPPI.
KEEP QUIET? BUT THEN AUNT LAURA MIGHT THINK I'M MAD AT HER.

SHE'S SPENT HER WHOLE LIFE AT SEA. POOR CHILD.
WELL...MMMM...OF COURSE, I COULD... MMMM...LET THE FOOD KEEP MY MOUTH SHUT...MMM.

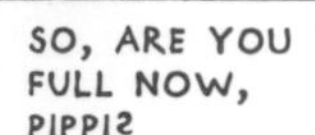
SO, ARE YOU FULL NOW, PIPPI?

NOPE. I'M NOT FULL. I'M THIRSTY.

LESS IS MORE, BUT YOU SURE DON'T HAVE MUCH TO EAT HERE.

WHAT AWFUL MANNERS YOU HAVE, MY DEAR. I DON'T THINK YOU'LL EVER BE A FINE LADY WHEN YOU GROW UP.
WE'LL JUST HAVE TO HOPE FOR THE BEST. I WAS ACTUALLY THINKING OF BECOMING A FINE PIRATE.

BUT WHAT IF I DO TURN OUT TO BE A FINE LADY WITH A VEIL AND THREE DOUBLE CHINS? OH NO!

HOW HAVE YOU BEEN LATELY, AUNT LAURA?
NOT GOOD. I'M ANXIOUS AND NERVOUS ALL THE TIME.
JUST LIKE MY GRANDMA. IF SHE'S OUT ON THE STREET AND A ROOF TILE FALLS ON HER HEAD, SHE STARTS JUMPING AND SCREAMING. YOU'D THINK SHE'D BEEN IN AN ACCIDENT.

YOU DON'T HAVE A GRANDMA, PIPPI.

THAT'S RIGHT. I DON'T. SO YOU'D THINK SHE COULD RELAX A BIT.

JUST IMAGINE: YESTERDAY, THE STRANGEST THING HAPPENED TO ME...
SPEAKING OF STRANGE THINGS HAPPENING...

MY FATHER ONCE HIRED A SAILOR NAMED AGATON—THE UGLIEST MAN IN THE WORLD. HE WAS PIGEON-TOED WITH JET-BLACK HAIR AND ONLY ONE TOOTH IN HIS MOUTH. PAPPA SAID HE COULD EVEN SCARE OFF A HORSE.

AND BELIEVE IT OR NOT, THEN WE GOT ANOTHER SAILOR NAMED TEODOR.
REALLY? WHAT DID HE LOOK LIKE?

EXACTLY THE SAME. THOSE TWO WERE LIKE TWINS. ESPECIALLY TEODOR.

HOW PECULIAR.
WHAT'S PECULIAR ABOUT THAT? THEY WERE TWINS, AFTER ALL.

THEY WERE? THEN WHY ARE YOU TALKING ABOUT STRANGE THINGS HAPPENING?

BECAUSE THEY WERE PIGEON-TOED. SO THEIR RIGHT BIG TOE BUMPED INTO THE LEFT. ISN'T THAT STRANGE? THEIR BIG TOES THOUGHT SO, ANYWAY.

PAPPA WAS SO HAPPY WHEN WE GOT TEODOR, BECAUSE THE TWO OF THEM COULD SCARE OFF TWICE AS MANY HORSES.

Pippi gets a letter
I'M SORRY, PIPPI, YOU CAN'T SEE TOMMY AND ANNIKA TODAY. THEY HAVE THE MEASLES.

NO MEASLES CAN EVER GET ME.

UGH, HOW BORING IT IS TO BE SICK!

WHEN PEOPLE ARE SICK, YOU NEED TO HOIST UP SOME TREATS FOR THEM.

OH, HOW NICE PIPPI IS!

WHEN PEOPLE ARE SICK, YOU NEED TO HOIST YOURSELF UP TO SEE THEM.

AND THEN IT'S GOOD TO SHOW THEM A FEW TRICKS.

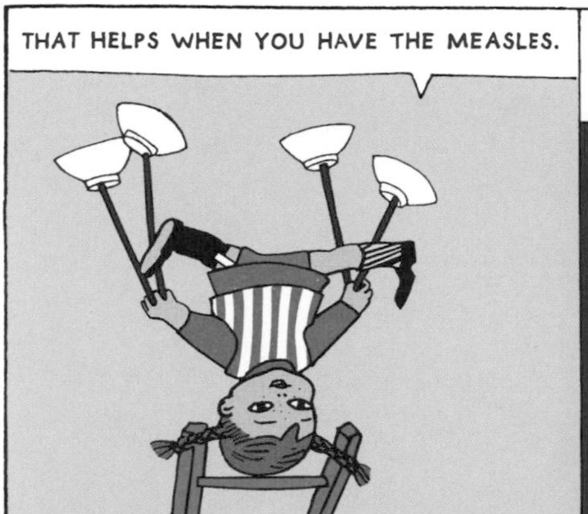
THAT HELPS WHEN YOU HAVE THE MEASLES.

HELLO, UP THERE! ARE YOU PIPPI LONGSTOCKING?

YES. WHO DID YOU THINK I WAS? THE EMPRESS OF ABYSSINIA?

HERE'S A LETTER FOR YOU.
FOR ME? A LEAL RETTER... I MEAN, A REAL LETTER?

I THINK IT'S FROM PAPPA. WHAT ON EARTH COULD HE WANT?

Dear Pippi,
Since your father is a South Seas king, you need to visit him now and then. So I'm sending you my boat to bring you here. Everyone is looking forward to meeting princess Pippilotta, and your father is too.
King Ephraim I Longstocking,
ruler of Kurrakurradoot Island.

Pippi goes on board again
PRINCESS OF KURRAKURRADOOT ISLAND.
IT'S GOING TO BE GREAT!

I THINK IT'LL BE FUN TO PLAY WITH
THOSE SOUTH SEAS ISLAND KIDS.

AND YOU'LL GET TO CLIMB PALM TREES,
MR. NILSSON. AND TOSS COCONUTS
TO THE GROUND.

WHAT'S WRONG WITH YOU TWO? DON'T
YOU LIKE SOUTH SEAS ISLAND KIDS?
WE'RE SAD BECAUSE YOU'RE LEAVING
US. DON'T YOU KNOW THAT?

WHO SAYS I'M LEAVING YOU?
BUT DIDN'T YOU SAY THAT YOU'RE GOING TO SEA?
SURE, BUT I'M NOT LEAVING YOU. YOU'RE COMING WITH ME, OF COURSE.
MAMMA WILL NEVER LET US GO.
SURE SHE WILL.
HURRAY!
HURRAY! SOON THE HOPPETOSSA WILL COME TO PICK US UP. HURRAY!

HI, PAPPA EPHRAIM! HOW ARE YOU?
HOPPETOSSA

ARE YOU CRAZY? YOU'RE LETTING YOUR CHILDREN GO TO THE SOUTH SEAS WITH PIPPI LONGSTOCKING?
IT'S OKAY. PIPPI MAY ACT A BIT STRANGE, BUT SHE'S THE NICEST CHILD IN THE WORLD.

BE CAREFUL NOT TO FALL IN.

HEY, LITTLE HORSEY. IF YOU GET SEASICK, YOU CAN JUST CLIMB THE MAST. THAT ALWAYS HELPS.

ONE, TWO, THREE...WE'RE OFF TO THE SOUTH SEAS!

YES, NOW WE'RE HOISTING THE SAIL.

WHEN YOU REACH THE NORTH SEA, YOU NEED TO PUT ON TWO UNDERSHIRTS. DON'T FORGET!

I HAVE SUCH A STRANGE FEELING. WHEN I GROW UP, I THINK I'M GOING TO BE A PIRATE, TOO.

Pippi at sea
HEY, WHAT A BLUSTERY DAY IT IS!

PIPPI, I GET SCARED WHEN THE WIND BLOWS SO HARD.
BLOWS SO HARD? THE SHIP'S CAT STILL HAS HER FUR, SO YOU CAN'T SAY IT'S BLOWING HARD.

I'D CALL THIS A FRESH BREEZE. IT'S NOT A REAL GALE UNLESS PAPPA GETS BLOWN INTO THE SEA OR SOMETHING LIKE THAT...

MAN OVER-BOARD!
WHAT?! THERE HE GOES!

HELP!
I CAN'T SWIM!!
I GUESS IT'S A REAL GALE AFTER ALL.
HOPP

RELAX! CALM DOWN!

RELAX, PAPPA. I HAVE A CERTIFICATE IN LIFE-SAVING, WEIGHT-LIFTING, AND FINGER-PULLING.

AHOY! OVER HERE!

THANKS FOR PULLING ME OUT OF THE DRINK, PIPPI.
OH, IT WAS NOTHING!

THIS CALLS FOR A CELEBRATION, FRIDOLF. BRING THE CREAM CAKE...

AND THE PYRAMID CAKE...

AND... THE LEMONADE...

AND SOME MEATBALLS...

AND TASTY LITTLE SAUSAGES...

AND ANOTHER CREAM CAKE...
AYE, AYE, CAPTAIN!

SOMETIMES IT'S GOOD TO GET CAUGHT IN A REAL GALE!

Pippi goes ashore
KURRAKURRADOOT DEAD AHEAD!

USSAMKURA KUSSOMKARA!

WHAT DOES THAT MEAN?
IT MEANS: "WELCOME BACK, ISLAND KING."

NAGORA FILLAROOTTAN!
EXACTLY.

WHAT DOES THAT MEAN?
IT MEANS: "STRONG PRINCESS, CAN YOU REALLY LIFT A HORSE?"

AMAZING, BUT I CAN. I CAN ALSO LIFT YOUR BIG ISLAND KING.

FILLAROOTTAN LEI.

KING EPHRAIM I LONGSTOCKING. HEE, HEE!
NOW I'D BETTER GET BACK TO RULING.

WHY ARE YOU ALL BOWING LIKE THAT?
YOU'RE A VERY GRAND LITTLE PRINCESS.

AND YOU'RE A VERY GRAND LITTLE RASCAL. COME ON, LET'S GO PLAY.

WE'RE MAKING A CAMPFIRE ON THE SOUTH SEAS BEACH.

HERE ARE BANANAS FROM MOMO.

HERE ARE COCONUTS FROM MOANA.

AND TONIGHT YOU CAN SLEEP IN THIS BAMBOO HUT.

AND HERE ARE FLOWERS FROM MUMRIK.

AND NOBODY HAS TO DO PLUTIFICATION TODAY...JUST THINK OF THAT!
HEY, FILLAROOTTAN LEI!

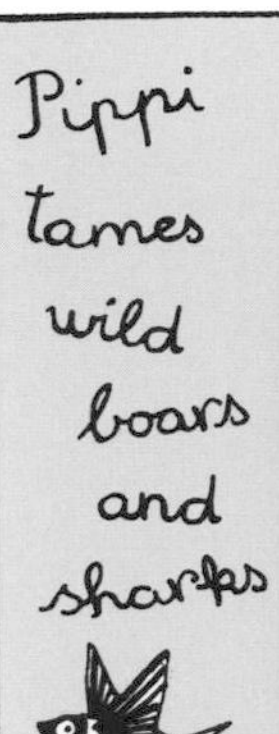
Pippi tames wild boars and sharks

WHY ARE ALL OF YOU LEAVING THE ISLAND?
WE'RE GOING ON A WILD BOAR HUNT ON ANOTHER ISLAND. THE KIDS HAVE TO STAY HOME. DOES THAT WORRY YOU?

THREE GUESSES! BUT AREN'T THERE ANY WILD BOAR HERE THAT YOU COULD HUNT?
NOPE, NOT EVEN A TINY PIGLET.

YOU KIDS WANT TO SEE NICE CAVES? YES? NO?

OF COURSE WE WANT TO SEE NICE CAVES. YUP, WE SURE DO!

NICE CAVE UP THERE. YOU KIDS WANT TO CLIMB?
YIKES. I DON'T DARE. WHAT IF I FALL INTO THE SEA?

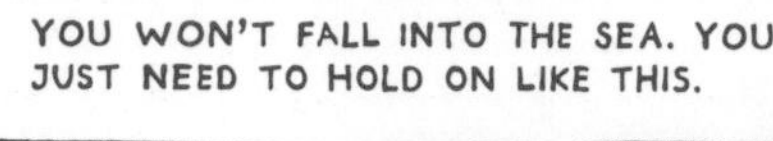
YOU WON'T FALL INTO THE SEA. YOU JUST NEED TO HOLD ON LIKE THIS.

SHARK! SHARK!
HELP!

BEAT IT! WERE YOU THINKING OF EATING TOMMY? SHAME ON YOU!

ARE YOU CRYING BECAUSE TOMMY ALMOST DIED?
NO, I'M CRYING BECAUSE THAT POOR LITTLE SHARK WON'T GET ANY BREAKFAST TODAY.

OH, PIPPI! A WILD BOAR!
GET OUT OF HERE! YOU DON'T EXIST. THAT'S WHAT PAPPA SAID.

BEAT IT! YOU DON'T EXIST...IS THAT SO HARD TO UNDERSTAND?

UH-OH...MAYBE YOU DO EXIST AFTER ALL.

IN THAT CASE, I THINK YOU SHOULD STAY UP THERE AND CALM DOWN A COUPLE OF NOTCHES.

Pippi becomes a cave-dweller
WHAT A NICE CAVE WE HAVE!

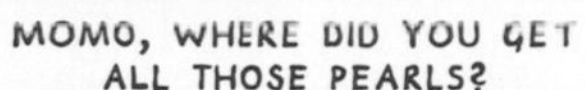
MOMO, WHERE DID YOU GET ALL THOSE PEARLS?

ALL THE KIDS FISH OYSTERS OUT OF THE SEA.

REAL PEARLS ARE THE BEST FOR PLAYING MARBLES...THAT'S WHAT MY GRANDPA ALWAYS SAID.

A STEAMBOAT? THAT'S ODD.

THE KIDS ON THIS ISLAND USE REAL PEARLS TO PLAY MARBLES. CAN YOU BELIEVE IT?
WE'LL CHANGE THEIR MINDS ABOUT THAT.
LOOK! THERE ARE THE KIDS!
WE'LL TELL THEM WE'RE JUST HERE TO GO SWIMMING.
IS THIS A GOOD PLACE TO SWIM?
SURE. FOR SHARKS.
YOU CAN'T FOOL ME. THERE AREN'T ANY SHARKS HERE.
THEN WHAT DO YOU CALL THAT? A TROUT?

HELP! HELP! A SHARK!

I TOLD YOU THIS WAS A GOOD PLACE FOR SHARKS TO SWIM.

HEY, KIDS, DO YOU HAVE ANY PEARLS UP THERE?
YES. ABOUT FIVE OR SIX QUARTS OF THEM.

GREAT. I'M COMING UP TO GET THEM.

HELP! A SHARK!

COCONUTS ARE GOOD FOR SCARING OFF SHARKS. THAT'S WHAT GRANDPA ALWAYS SAID.

SORRY. I THOUGHT YOU WERE A SHARK.

ARE YOU TRYING TO KILL ME?

Pippi talks sense into Buck and Jim
IF YOU DON'T GIVE US THOSE PEARLS, YOU'LL HAVE TO STAY UP THERE IN THE CAVE UNTIL YOU STARVE TO DEATH.
THAT WON'T HAPPEN UNTIL THE FALL OF 2099.

BECAUSE WE'VE GOT SO MANY COCONUTS.

IF YOU DON'T BRING US THOSE PEARLS, WE'RE GOING TO KILL YOUR HORSE.

WATCH OUT OR I'LL GET AS MAD AS GRANDPA.

MY GRANDPA GOT SO MAD THAT HE BIT OFF HIS OWN NOSE.

HA. NOBODY CAN BITE OFF HIS OWN NOSE.
YOU CAN IF YOU CLIMB ONTO A CHAIR. THAT'S WHAT GRANDPA DID.

BUT PIPPI, YOU DON'T HAVE A GRANDPA.
I DON'T. DO I REALLY NEED ONE?

WHAT DID YOU SAY YOU WOULD DO TO MY HORSE?

IF YOU DON'T GIVE US THOSE PEARLS, WE'RE GOING TO KILL HIM.
I'LL COUNT TO THREE. THEN WE'LL WHACK HIM.

SAME HERE. ONE, TWO, THREE, THEN I'LL WHACK YOU.
WHACKING ONE...
WHACKING TWO...

WHACKING BOTH OF YOU.

YOU CAN PLAY MARBLES SOME OTHER TIME. NOW OFF YOU GO TO MAMMA.

MY HORSEY!

HURRAY! PIPPI IS THE STRONGEST IN THE WORLD.

Pippi goes home
PIPPI, I WANT TO GO HOME TO MAMMA.
ME TOO.

DON'T YOU WANT TO PICK ANY MORE COCONUTS?

AND SWING ON THE BAMBOO SWING?

AND DIVE FOR PEARLS?

AND DANCE THE HULA-HULA? AND GET LOTS OF PRETTY FRECKLES ON YOUR NOSE AND SAND BETWEEN YOUR TOES?

NO, WE'D RATHER GO HOME TO MAMMA.

PAPPA, I'M THINKING OF GOING HOME TO VILLA VILLEKULLA. WHAT DO YOU SAY TO THAT?
GO IN PEACE, MY DEAR CHILD.

GOODBYE, GOODBYE, GOODBYE, GOODBYE. WE'LL COME BACK SOON.

SOON WE'LL REACH THE NORTH SEA, SO WE'D BETTER GET OUT OUR UNDERSHIRTS.
DO YOU THINK WE'LL BE HOME BY CHRISTMAS, PIPPI?

GANGWAY! HERE COME THE SWEDES!

WOW, LOOK AT ALL THE SNOW. WHAT FUN!
BUT IT'S NOT SO FUN THAT WE DIDN'T GET HERE BY CHRISTMAS. NOW WE WON'T HAVE ANY CHRISTMAS PRESENTS.

PIPPI, YOU CAN'T STAY IN VILLA VILLEKULLA TONIGHT. YOU'LL FREEZE TO DEATH.
AS LONG AS YOU HAVE A WARM HEART, YOU'LL NEVER FREEZE.

WELL, GOOD NIGHT, DEAR, SWEET PIPPI. SEE YOU TOMORROW.
OKAY. SAY HELLO TO YOUR MAMMA AND PAPPA.

WELCOME HOME, DEAR CHILDREN.

TOMORROW I'LL HAVE TO SHOVEL THE SNOW.

I'M NOT COLD AT ALL. BUT THAT'S BECAUSE THERE ARE NO COLD FEET UNDER THE BLANKET WITH ME.

Pippi won't grow up ...
WHAT A SHAME THAT WE DIDN'T GET HOME FOR CHRISTMAS.
I KNOW. IT'S REALLY SAD. BUT LET'S GO SEE PIPPI.

MERRY CHRISTMAS. WELCOME TO MY HUMBLE HOME.
CHRISTMAS? WHAT DO YOU MEAN?

THREE GUESSES! DO YOU THINK I MEAN EASTER?

WOW! A CHRISTMAS TREE AND EVERYTHING! WE DIDN'T MISS CHRISTMAS AFTER ALL!

DID YOU THINK YOU WOULD?
BUT NO CHRISTMAS PRESENTS, OF COURSE.

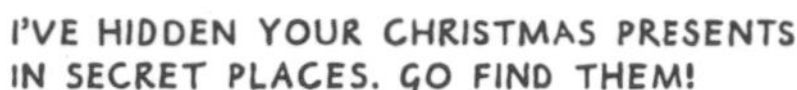
I'VE HIDDEN YOUR CHRISTMAS PRESENTS IN SECRET PLACES. GO FIND THEM!

LOOK! THERE'S A PRESENT FOR ME HANGING UP THERE.
AND HERE'S ONE FOR ME.

THANK YOU, DEAR, SWEET PIPPI! YOU'RE THE NICEST PERSON IN THE WHOLE WORLD.
HMM...I HEAR THERE'S SOMEONE IN FARAWAY INDIA WHO'S ALSO REALLY NICE.

OH, I NEVER WANT TO GROW UP.
BECAUSE THEN YOU'LL HAVE TO THINK OF BUNIONS AND COUNTY TAXES AND BORING STUFF LIKE THAT.

BUT THERE ARE PILLS YOU CAN TAKE SO YOU DON'T GROW UP. I HAVE THREE OF THEM HERE.
PEAS?

THAT'S WHAT YOU THINK! THEY'RE KRUMALURA PILLS. IF YOU EAT ONE OF THESE YOU CAN KEEP ON PLAYING UNTIL YOU'RE A HUNDRED.

HERE'S WHAT YOU SAY: DEAR LITTLE KRUMALURA, I DON'T WANT TO GROW UP. NEVER EVER.

DEAR LITTLE KRUMALURA, I DON'T WANT TO GROW UP. NEVER EVER.

HURRAY! NOW WE CAN PLAY WITH PIPPI FOREVER.

NOW WE CAN PLAY AND PLAY AND PLAY ALL DAY, FOR AS LONG AS WE LIVE. AND IN THE NIGHTTIME TOO.

Astrid Lindgren (1907–2002) was an immensely popular children's book author as well as a lifelong philanthropist. Her Pippi Longstocking series—*Pippi Longstocking* (1945), *Pippi Goes On Board* (1946), *Do You Know Pippi Longstocking?* (1947), and *Pippi in the South Seas* (1948)—has been translated into more than sixty languages and published all over the world.

During the winter of 1941, Lindgren's seven-year-old daughter Karin was ill and asked her mother to tell her a story about Pippi Longstocking. The story Astrid Lindgren told delighted Karin and all her friends. A few years later, while recovering from an injury, Lindgren finally found the time to write down the Pippi stories. Lindgren's tenth birthday present to her daughter was the completed Pippi manuscript.

Lindgren submitted a revised version of the manuscript to the annual Rabén & Sjögren writing contest, where it won first prize. The book was published in December of 1945, and became an instant success. Rabén & Sjögren hired Lindgren as a children's book editor in 1946; she was soon put in charge of their children's book imprint, where she worked for many years. As one of the world's best loved writers, Astrid Lindgren has written more than seventy novels and storybooks, with over 145 million books sold worldwide.

Ingrid Vang Nyman (1916–1959) was a Danish-born illustrator who was best known for her work on Swedish children's books. As a child, she suffered from tuberculosis, and at age thirteen, she lost vision in one eye.

Vang Nyman studied at the Royal Danish Academy of Fine Arts in Copenhagen before she moved to Stockholm, where her career in children's book illustration took off. She was briefly married to the poet and painter Arne Nyman, with whom she had a son named Peder. When the marriage ended in 1944, Ingrid Vang Nyman began a relationship with the lawyer and author Uno Eng. It was also around this time that she created the first images of Pippi Longstocking. Without a doubt, the feisty Pippi is somewhat of a kindred spirit with Vang Nyman, who had a strong faith in her own abilities—something not especially common among children's book illustrators of the day. Ingrid Vang Nyman went on to illustrate numerous children's books over the course of her brief career.

Tiina Nunnally is widely considered to be the preeminent translator of Scandinavian languages into English. Her many awards and honors include the PEN/BOMC Translation Prize for her work on Sigrid Undset's *Kristin Lavransdatter*. She grew up in Milwaukee and received an M.A. in Scandinavian Studies from the University of Wisconsin.